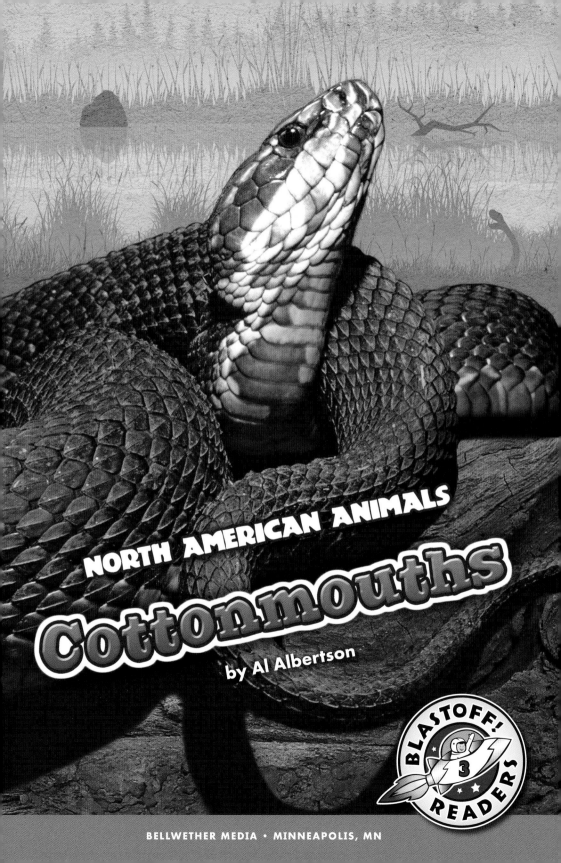

NORTH AMERICAN ANIMALS

Cottonmouths

by Al Albertson

BLASTOFF!
READERS
3

BELLWETHER MEDIA • MINNEAPOLIS, MN

Note to Librarians, Teachers, and Parents:

Blastoff! Readers are carefully developed by literacy experts and combine standards-based content with developmentally appropriate text.

Level 1 provides the most support through repetition of high-frequency words, light text, predictable sentence patterns, and strong visual support.

Level 2 offers early readers a bit more challenge through varied simple sentences, increased text load, and less repetition of high-frequency words.

Level 3 advances early-fluent readers toward fluency through increased text and concept load, less reliance on visuals, longer sentences, and more literary language.

Level 4 builds reading stamina by providing more text per page, increased use of punctuation, greater variation in sentence patterns, and increasingly challenging vocabulary.

Level 5 encourages children to move from "learning to read" to "reading to learn" by providing even more text, varied writing styles, and less familiar topics.

Whichever book is right for your reader, Blastoff! Readers are the perfect books to build confidence and encourage a love of reading that will last a lifetime!

This edition first published in 2020 by Bellwether Media, Inc.

No part of this publication may be reproduced in whole or in part without written permission of the publisher. For information regarding permission, write to Bellwether Media, Inc., Attention: Permissions Department, 6012 Blue Circle Drive, Minnetonka, MN 55343.

Library of Congress Cataloging-in-Publication Data

Names: Albertson, Al, author.
Title: Cottonmouths / by Al Albertson.
Description: Minneapolis, MN : Bellwether Media, Inc., [2020] | Series: Blastoff! Readers. North American Animals | Audience: Age 5-8. | Audience: K to Grade 3. | Includes bibliographical references and index.
Identifiers: LCCN 2018050651 (print) | LCCN 2018051501 (ebook) | ISBN 9781618915238 (ebook) | ISBN 9781626179837 (hardcover : alk. paper)
Subjects: LCSH: Agkistrodon piscivorus–Juvenile literature.
Classification: LCC QL666.O69 (ebook) | LCC QL666.O69 A43 2020 (print) | DDC 597.96–dc23
LC record available at https://lccn.loc.gov/2018050651

Editor: Kate Moening   Designer: Laura Sowers
Printed in the United States of America, North Mankato, MN.

Table of **Contents**

What Are Cottonmouths?	4
Colors of a Cottonmouth	8
A Deadly Bite	14
Slithering Snakelets	18
Glossary	22
To Learn More	23
Index	24

Cottonmouths are the only **venomous** water snakes in North America. These **reptiles** are sometimes called water moccasins.

In the Wild

N
W   E
S

Extinct

Extinct in the Wild

Critically Endangered

Endangered

Vulnerable

Near Threatened

Least Concern

cottonmouth range = ▣
conservation status: least concern

They live in wetlands throughout the southeastern United States.

Cottonmouths swim near the surface in calm waters. On land, they **slither** through fields to find new homes.

Cottonmouths like to warm up in the sun. They rest on logs or low tree branches.

Colors of a Cottonmouth

scales

Cottonmouths are covered in brown, black, or yellow **scales**. Dark bands wrap around their bodies. These bands usually fade with age.

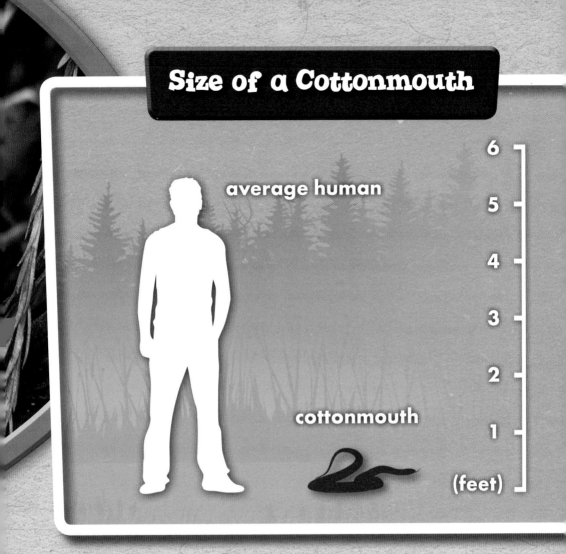

Size of a Cottonmouth

average human

cottonmouth

6
5
4
3
2
1
(feet)

Adult cottonmouths can be 2 to 6 feet (0.6 to 1.8 meters) long.

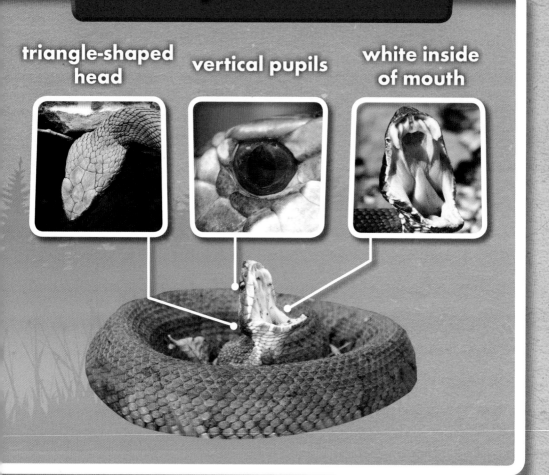

triangle-shaped head

vertical pupils

white inside of mouth

Cottonmouths have large, triangle-shaped heads. Their **pupils** are **vertical**.

coiling

These snakes **coil** and open
their mouths wide when they
are scared! The insides of their
mouths are white, like cotton.
That is how they got their name.

Small cottonmouths often become **prey**. Raccoons, snapping turtles, and birds hunt them.

Animals to Avoid

American alligators

great blue herons

common snapping turtles

raccoons

Cottonmouths hide if a **predator** is near. Their dark colors blend in with their surroundings. They can also release a terrible smell to escape!

Cottonmouths are **carnivores**. They eat fish, frogs, turtles, and other small animals.

Like other **vipers**, cottonmouths can sense heat. This helps them find warm prey.

fang

Cottonmouths release venom through their large **fangs**. Then the snakes open wide to swallow their prey whole!

American bullfrogs

bullhead catfish

ring-necked snakes

eastern mud turtles

Cottonmouth venom is very strong. It can be deadly to small animals and humans!

Slithering Snakelets

When it is time to **breed**, male cottonmouths fight over females. They try to slam each other to the ground. **Snakelets** grow in eggs inside their mom. Then females give birth to live babies!

Baby Facts

Name for babies:	snakelets
Size of litter:	up to 20
Length of pregnancy:	5 months
Time spent with mom:	up to a few days

snakelets

Females give birth every two or three years. They may stay with the babies for a few days after birth.

When the snakelets can move around on their own, they slither off into the world!

Glossary

breed—to produce offspring

carnivores—animals that only eat meat

coil—to form a series of loops

fangs—long, sharp teeth

predator—an animal that hunts other animals for food

prey—animals that are hunted by other animals for food

pupils—the small dark area in the center of the eye that makes it possible to see

reptiles—cold-blooded animals that have backbones and lay eggs

scales—small plates of skin that cover and protect a snake's body

slither—to move by smoothly sliding back and forth

snakelets—baby cottonmouths

venomous—having or producing venom, a poison created by cottonmouths

vertical—going straight up and down

vipers—venomous snakes with long fangs that can fold up

To Learn More

AT THE LIBRARY

Kenney, Karen Latchana. *Life Cycle of a Snake*. Minneapolis, Minn.: Pogo, 2019.

Kim, Carol. *Pit Viper*. Vero Beach, Fla.: Rourke Educational Media, 2018.

Lawrence, Ellen. *Cottonmouth*. New York, N.Y.: Bearport Publishing, 2017.

ON THE WEB

FACTSURFER

Factsurfer.com gives you a safe, fun way to find more information.

1. Go to www.factsurfer.com.

2. Enter "cottonmouths" into the search box and click 🔍.

3. Select your book cover to see a list of related web sites.

Index

bands, 8

branches, 7

breed, 18

carnivores, 14

coil, 11

colors, 8, 10, 11, 13

fangs, 16

females, 18, 20

fields, 6

heads, 10

hide, 13

logs, 7

males, 18

mouths, 10, 11

name, 4, 11

predator, 12, 13

prey, 12, 14, 15, 16, 17

pupils, 10

range, 5

reptiles, 4

rest, 7

scales, 8

size, 9

slither, 6, 21

smell, 13

snakelets, 18, 19, 20, 21

status, 5

swim, 6

United States, 5

venom, 4, 16, 17

vipers, 15

waters, 6

wetlands, 5

The images in this book are reproduced through the courtesy of: James H Robinson/ Getty, front cover; Mark Kostich, pp. 4-5, 21; jo Crebbin, pp. 6-7; Jonathan A. Maue, p. 7; Ira Mark Rappaport, pp. 8-9; Shackleford Photography, p. 10 (top left); Rob Hainer, p. 10 (top right); Coy St. Clair/ Getty, p. 10 (middle); Coy St. Clair, p. 11; Jay Ondreicka, pp. 12-13; reptiles4all, p. 13 (top left); Tathoms, p. 13 (top right); Arvind Balaraman, p. 13 (bottom left); Eric Isselee, p. 13 (bottom right); Paul S. Wolf, pp. 14-15, 18-19; tornado98, p. 15; Seth LaGrange, pp. 16-17; JIANG HONGYAN, p. 17 (top left); Rostislav Stefanek, p. 17 (top right); IrinaK, p. 17 (bottom left); fivespots, p. 17 (bottom right); Spiraling Road Photography/ Getty, p. 19; Barry Freeman/ Alamy, p. 20.